GLOW IN THE DARK:
ANIMALS AT
NIGHT

written by
KATY FLINT

illustrated by
CORNELIA LI

WIDE EYED EDITIONS

OPOSSUMS hide out in places like tree burrows and attics. When threatened, they can pretend to be dead. Leave them alone and they will eventually wake up.

RACCOONS eat just about anything—so are highly adapted to life in a busy city. These clever masked bandits have specials paws that allow them to open things like jars, locks, and trash cans.

102

SKUNK

CITY

At night, when most children are going to sleep, some animals start to wake up. Many come out at dusk, as the sky darkens, or at dawn, when the sun's rays start to light up the night sky. Some wait until it is pitch black to come out from their cozy dens and nests. All of these animals are active at night for a reason. Some prefer the cooler air, or the hunting opportunities. Some are safer at night from predators. Nighttime animals have special senses, such as excellent hearing or a keen sense of smell, to help them survive in the dark. So, let's go on a journey around the world, to meet the animals that come out at night— starting in the city.

Your HOUSE CAT is most active at dawn and dusk.

MICE usually come out at night. They have poor eyesight but a very good sense of hearing and smell. They also have long whiskers to sense air movements and touch surfaces.

RAIN FOREST

JAGUARS have jaws that are so strong, they can crack a turtle shell. They also have beautiful rosettes and spots on their coat.

Deep in the South American rain forest, the jaguar stalks its prey. The shadows of the night allow it to creep up and pounce on creatures from the trees. Elsewhere, a boa constrictor slithers through the forest, tightening its coils around a branch. Up in the trees, the sloth moves so slowly, it's hard to tell if it is even awake at all. It grasps the tree with its long claws as its baby clings to its belly.

BOA
CONSTRICTOR

KINKAJOUS love
fruit and also slurp
nectar from flowers
with their very
long tongues. They
come out at night
and nest in tree
hollows in the day.

THREE-TOED
SLOTH

NIGHT MONKEYS have large
brown eyes, which help them
see in the dark. They are the
only monkeys to come out at
night. They are also known as
"owl monkeys" because of
their large eyes.

You may not expect to see them on the beach, but in some areas, RED FOXES creep up and try to snatch hatchlings from their nests.

Female TURTLES use the Earth's magnetic field to find their way across the wide oceans back to the beach where they hatched out of their eggs. They then lay their own eggs on the same beach.

LOGGERHEAD HATCHLINGS

Mother turtles use their flippers to dig a deep hole in the sand. They lay 80 to 100 eggs in each nest hole.

BEACH

The turtle hatchlings follow the bright light of the moon into the sea.

GHOST CRABS

When the moonlight sparkles on the ocean waves, baby turtles make a break for the open sea. They climb out of their sandy nests on an Australian beach, trying to make it to the safety of the ocean. They do this at night to avoid the predatory seabirds of the daytime. However, some predators, such as crabs, are awake and try to pick off the baby turtles as they scramble to the sea. The ones that make it paddle furiously to deeper waters, where they will be safe.

BOOBOOK
OWL

DINGOES are
the wild dogs of
Australia. They are
most active at dawn
and dusk, when they
hunt for prey such
as rabbits, mice,
birds, and lizards.
Their keen sense of
smell helps them to
find their prey.

In the dingo den, a female
has given birth to a litter
of pups. The whole pack
helps to raise them.

SHORT-BEAKED
ECHIDNA

OUTBACK

As the sun sets on the red rocks of the outback, many Australian animals become active. Daytime temperatures can reach up to 113 degrees Fahrenheit, so lots of creatures come out at night, when it is much cooler. Kangaroos hop over the parched earth at speeds of 25 miles per hour, pushing off from the ground with their powerful back legs. Dingoes come out of their den to hunt, either alone, or together as a pack. The boobook owl calls "boo-book" into the night, while long-eared bats leave their daytime roost.

LONG-EARED BATS

RED KANGAROO

NIGHT PARROTS are rare and mysterious birds. They emerge after sunset to feed on the ground on the seeds of spinifex bushes. Their yellow and green feathers provide good camouflage among the bushes.

BILBYS do not need to drink water because they get all the moisture they need from food, such as insects and seeds. They have a very long, sticky tongue to lick up seeds!

FLYING
SQUIRREL

LUNA MOTHS live for only one or
two weeks after they emerge from
their cocoon. Their cocoon is made
from silk and leaves. Look out for
the eyespots on their wings.

BADGERS have
an excellent
sense of smell,
sight, and
hearing.

WOODLAND

It is a warm summer evening in the woodlands of North America. Green leaves flutter on the trees and fireflies twinkle like fairy lights. An American badger snuffles through the forest glade, looking for small animals to eat, such as squirrels and mice. A pair of luna moths fly past; their bright green wings seem to glow. Look out for the gray fox, with its peppering of gray and cinnamon-colored fur. This fox is the only fox that can climb trees. Up in the trees, it can escape predators, find food, and sleep in tree hollows.

GRAY FOXES have sharp, curved claws that allow them to dig dens, capture their prey, climb trees, and protect themselves from predators, like coyotes, bobcats, owls, and golden eagles.

FIREFLIES are night-active beetles. They use a chemical reaction to make light at the end of their abdomen. Fireflies flash their lights in a particular pattern to attract a mate.

EURASIAN EAGLE OWLS make a ghostly hooting noise as they call out into the darkness to attract a mate. However, they are not scary but shy creatures that are now endangered.

WOLVES communicate using coded howls and body language. The wolf pack is led by the two toughest wolves—a top male and a top female.

LEMMING

Look out for the NORTHERN LIGHTS (*aurora borealis*) glowing green in the sky while you're here.

In summer, the ARCTIC FOX'S coat will turn brown.

ARCTIC

In the frozen Arctic, winter conditions are harsh. The Arctic fox grows a coat as white as the snow that covers the ground, which allows it to blend in with its surroundings. It hears its next meal, a lemming, underneath the snow pack and leaps down from on high to break through the snow. In the distance, a wolf pack howls. This lets any other wolf know that this is their territory. Meanwhile, the eagle owl looks on from its hiding place in a tree hollow. It's time for it to spread its wings and swoop down on prey.

MOUNTAINS

The puma has long back legs, which enable it to jump as high as 18 feet upward and 40 feet forward. Their large, strong paws help them to grip slippery rocks and travel through deep snow as if they are wearing snowshoes.

PUMAS do not have traditional dens, but find different nurseries every night for their cubs.

PUMA CUBS have spotted patterns on their coats for camouflage.

High in the Andes mountain range lives the golden-coated puma. People call it the "lion of the Andes" around here. It is now springtime and the snow is starting to melt. The mother has given birth to two cubs. As night falls, it is time for her to leave the nursery and go off to hunt. She stalks the local guanacos, a herd of llama-like creatures. If she catches and kills one, she will save it and eat it in the morning.

PUMAS are also known as ghost cats, as they are really hard to find.

GUANACOS

SKUNK

MANGROVE

In the mangrove forest, all is eerily still. But one creature is on the prowl. The Bengal tiger is the jewel of the mangrove forest. It slips quietly into the water and swims, looking for prey with its special reflective eyes. At night, this tangled forest of tree roots and water channels takes on a magical appearance. All looks inky black, apart from tiny drifting plants and animals, called plankton, which glow every time the tiger paddles along with its powerful legs.

INDIAN TREE FROGS are active at night when the air is humid. This helps them to keep their skin moist, which they need to do in order to survive.

PLANKTON glow bright blue in the water. They give off light to startle, confuse, or scare away predators.

Look out for arches of finger-like MANGROVE ROOTS: a distinctive feature of any mangrove forest.

The SUNDERBANS MANGROVE SWAMP in India has the largest concentration of Bengal tigers in the world.

TIGERS are the largest big cat and the only big cat that likes to swim. They hunt at night, resting and grooming in the day.

RINGTAILS have flexible back feet, which are good for gripping as they climb. They can scale tall cacti and steep rocks.

BOBCATS have tiny, bobbed tails and short fur. They change their shelter every day, choosing rocky dens, boulders, caves, or hollow logs.

TARANTULAS hunt at night. They try to eat anything of a suitable size that wanders nearby: other spiders, beetles, grasshoppers, and even lizards!

DESERT

Spot the SAGUARO CACTUS, one of the most famous plants of this desert. It stores water inside its spongy stem and may weigh as much as an elephant when it's full of water.

On the rocky outcrops of the Sonoran Desert in Arizona, many animals become active before sunrise. The bobcat waits to ambush its prey: a diamondback rattlesnake. The snake rises up and shakes its famous tail in defense. Ringtails clamber up sharp rockfaces to escape the fight. The collared peccary makes snuffling, snorting sounds as it looks for plants to eat. They are all watched by the great horned owl, swooping silently through the cool night air.

GREAT
HORNED OWL

COLLARED
PECCARY

WESTERN
DIAMONDBACK
RATTLESNAKE

CORAL REEF

The Caribbean coral reef bursts into deep color at night. Corals absorb small amounts of light, which makes them glow in the dark. Many creatures work the night shift, while their plant-eating colleagues hide and sleep between rocks. Now is the time for predators to come out and hunt: schools of squirrelfish swim down to the seabed to feed on smaller fish. Watch out for the lone octopus feeling for hidden creatures. It reaches into every hole in the reef, smelling and tasting for prey with the suckers on its long tentacles. When sunlight begins to shine through the water, it will return to its cave to sleep.

PARROTFISH

The ALGAE living inside the corals need light to make food.

CORALS stretch out their stinging tentacles to catch tiny plants and animals (plankton) drifting past in the water.

SQUIRRELFISH spot prey, and predators, with their large eyes.

OCTOPUS

BRAIN CORAL

PUFFERFISH are protected by their sharp spines, which stick out when they puff up like a balloon at the first sign of danger.

SEA URCHINS use thousands of tiny, water-filled tube feet to crawl slowly over the seabed in search of algae to eat.

As day dawns on the African savanna, the creatures of the night head to bed. The aardvark burrows into its den to go to sleep. A pride of lions survey the savanna, before they prepare to sleep under an acacia tree—snuggling up with their playful cubs. Even the scorpion goes to bed. The sun rises and its rays beat down, heating up the dry, cracked earth. Our adventure is over and it's time for rest...until night draws in once more.

BLACK RHINO

HYENA

EMPEROR SCORPIONS hunt under the cover of darkness. They glow pastel blue under UV light.

AARDVARK

Lions love to eat PORCUPINES, but they have to get past the prickles first. The porcupine's sharp spines, called quills, protect it from becoming a lion's breakfast.

PANGOLIN

LIONS are most active at dawn and dusk. They are the only big cats to live in groups, called prides.

The female lions are the hunters and work together to bring down prey.

SAVANNA

For everyone who loves a bedtime story. —K.F.

To my parents, who are infinitely supportive on my journey. —C.L.

Inspiring | Educating | Creating | Entertaining

Brimming with creative inspiration, how-to projects, and useful information to enrich your everyday life, Quarto Knows is a favorite destination for those pursuing their interests and passions. Visit our site and dig deeper with our books into your area of interest: Quarto Creates, Quarto Cooks, Quarto Homes, Quarto Lives, Quarto Drives, Quarto Explores, Quarto Gifts, or Quarto Kids.

Glow in the Dark: Animals at Night © 2019 Quarto Publishing plc.
Illustrations by Cornelia Li. Written by Katy Flint.
Natural history consultation by Barbara Taylor.

First Published in 2019 by Wide Eyed Editions, an imprint of The Quarto Group.
400 First Avenue North, Suite 400, Minneapolis, MN 55401, USA.
T (612) 344-8100 F (612) 344-8692 **www.QuartoKnows.com**

A catalog record for this book is available from the British Library.

ISBN 978-1-78603-540-0

The illustrations were created digitally using hand-painted textures.
Set in Hipton Sans, Roboto Slab, and Apercu.

Published by Jenny Broom
Designed by Nicola Price
Production by Jenny Cundill
Manufactured in Guangdong, China CC042021
9 8 7 6 5 4 3 2